CRYING HELP

By Apostle Designate
Reshea Little

authorHOUSE®

AuthorHouse™
1663 Liberty Drive
Bloomington, IN 47403
www.authorhouse.com
Phone: 1 (800) 839-8640

Published by AuthorHouse   10/09/2015

ISBN: 978-1-5049-5464-8 (sc)
ISBN: 978-1-5049-5462-4 (hc)
ISBN: 978-1-5049-5463-1 (e)

Library of Congress Control Number: 2015916697

Print information available on the last page.

Any people depicted in stock imagery provided by Thinkstock are models,
and such images are being used for illustrative purposes only.
Certain stock imagery © Thinkstock.

This book is printed on acid-free paper.

Because of the dynamic nature of the Internet, any web addresses or links contained in
this book may have changed since publication and may no longer be valid. The views
expressed in this work are solely those of the author and do not necessarily reflect the
views of the publisher, and the publisher hereby disclaims any responsibility for them.

Scripture quotations marked KJV are from the Holy Bible, King James Version
(Authorized Version). First published in 1611. Quoted from the KJV Classic
Reference Bible, Copyright © 1983 by The Zondervan Corporation.

Cited Sources

The Free Dictionary

Life Application Bible – New living translation

King James Bible

Our Daily Bread

www.gotquestions.org

www.easyenglish.info

LaMonya George….Typist

Timothy "Antwan" Little…..Artist for Cover

Contents

Chapter 1 Need Help, Call For Assistance (Jesus) 1

Chapter 2 Struggling With Addictions 9

Chapter 3 How Long Shall I Wait.................................. 19

Chapter 4 Crybaby Blues 27

Chapter 5 Help Is On The Way 35

Chapter 6 Cry Help Thru Relationships........................ 45

Chapter 7 Let The Son Shine In.................................... 63

Chapter 8 My Testimony... 71

Chapter 9 Crying To Jesus (God)................................. 77

Special Thanks

To God our Father and our Lord and Saviour Jesus Christ, and our Comforter the Holy Ghost.

Thank you, to my husband Bishop Designate Timothy Little who pushes me to be the best woman, and who treats me like his Barbie doll, Yes, Barbie doll. You are my Love and Joy, the best Prophet I know, keep preaching and prophesying by the Grace of God. He is a true Prophet of God and my cupcake with icing on it.

And to my mother Catherine Flanagan, who I watched get up every morning at 5am to pray.

To my sisters: Valerie, Wanda, and Felicia,

And all our children; Mario, Pooh, Donta, Boo, Twan, Erica, Eric, etc.

Love and Peace be with you all!!!

Sisters and brothers: Valerie, Antonio, Alice, Richard, Angela, and Anthony

Joy in His Presence!!!

And a plethora (a large amount) of Grandchildren

Acknowledgements

I have been carrying some version of this book around in my head for almost 20 years. It all began when I started in Ministry preaching the word of God at God's Tabernacle of Praise under Pastor and Lady Billy & Charlene Woods for 19 years. In 1995, I received my license and then got ordained in 1996, then I experienced a lot of different situations in my life where crying played a large part. After a good cry, I always felt cleansed. Crying heals us physiologically, spiritually, and psychologically.

Then to our Chief Apostle Marion Johnson and Sr. Bishop Ralph Johnson who are our overseers, a special shout out to you for being the best spiritual parents anyone could ever have, because of you both, we are who we are and we have The Power of Faith to have Confidence in God's Word. Same Like Faith Family Christian Center and Same Like Faith Ebenezer, we thank God for your big push, and when I say big push that is exactly what I mean. You saw something in us to get us to where we are and where we are moving forward to years and counting. Well done, thou good and faithful servants, thou hast been faithful over a few things, I will make you ruler over many things; enter thou into the joy of thy Lord; As you continue to stay steadfast and unmovable in the things of God, greater works shall you do.

Love you Mom and Dad

Same Like Faith Ebenezer Ministries Fellowship International, Inc.

Same Like Faith Family Christian Center Church Inc.

Introduction

What makes you <u>cry</u>, and why does crying come easily to some people but others rarely shed a tear? Letting your emotions take hold of you, whether that results in crying or not, could <u>help</u> you find the reason behind your tears. How long has it been since you had a good cry? Some people see crying as a sign of weakness, but confronting your emotions requires strength in the form of vulnerability.

Crying can elevate mood. Do you know what your manganese levels are? Well neither do I. But chances are you will feel better if it's lower because over exposure to manganese can cause bad stuff, anxiety, nervousness, irritability, fatigue, etc. Grab a tissue if you need to and this book in its entirety. Help make it easier for someone to do something by offering one's service or resources; to give assistance. We all know a good cry helps to soothe our minds. Some doctors are discovering that tears may help to heal our bodies.

Crying lowers stress. Crying relieves stress and tears remove some of the chemicals built up in the body from stress. If we suppress our tears it increases stress levels and contributes to diseases associated with stress such as heart problems, high blood pressure and ulcers.

Tears release feelings. Even if you haven't just gone through something traumatic or are severely depressed, the average person goes through their day accumulating conflicts and resentments. Crying is cathartic; it lets the

devil out before they wreck all kind of havoc with the nervous and cardiovascular systems. We need to stomp and storm: to sob and cry: to perspire and tremble.

Psalm 46:1 – God is our refuge and strength, a very present help in trouble.

Psalm 46:5 – God is in the midst of her; she shall not be moved: God shall help her and that right early.

Crying is a release, release, release..........

Boo, hoo, hoo

CHAPTER 1

NEED HELP, CALL FOR ASSISTANCE (JESUS)

There are so many numbers we can call for Help: 411 for Information, 511 for Travel, traffic; 611 for Mobile help, and 911 for Emergencies. But we need to call 111 for The Father, Son, and Holy Ghost. 1 for the Father, 1 for the Son, and 1 for the Holy Ghost. Too many times we can feel helpless and out of control and God is perfectly able to help in our times of need. (Psalm 46:1) – "God is our refuge and strength, always ready to help in times of trouble."

Jonah was afraid, he knew that God had a specific job for him, but didn't want to do it. Isn't that just like us when God calls us to do a task, we try to run from it. I ran for a whole year when God called me to preach, I didn't want to do it either. When God gives us directions through His Word, sometimes we run in fear, claiming that God is asking too much of us. Fear made Jonah run, Fear made me run, but running gets us into worse trouble than before. For that year of running, I went thru hell. Everything I put my hands to do failed.

Boo, Hoo, Hoo……..

In the end Jonah knew that it was best to do what God had asked in the first place, but by then he had paid a costly price for running. It is far better to obey from the start. Read the book of Jonah Chapter 1-4 in its entirety. Jonah chapter 4:1-2, Jonah revealed the reason for his reluctance

to go Nineveh. He wanted the Ninevites destroyed, not forgiven, have any of us been like that, wanted people to be destroyed instead of saved. Jonah didn't understand that the God of Israel is also the God of the world.

Are we surprised when some unexpected person turns to God? Maybe your view is as narrow as Jonahs'. Don't forget that in reality that none of us deserves to be forgiven by God, but he is a forgiving God. He is faithful and just to forgive, and cleanses us from all unrighteous. Jonah chapter 4:9, Jonah was angry at the death of the plant, but not over what could have happened to Nineveh.

Most of us have cried at the death of a pet or an object with sentimental value is broken, but have we cried over a friend who does not know God? It is easy to be more sensitive to our own interest than to the spiritual needs of people around us. What are you sensitive to? Although the prophet Jonah tried to run away from God, God was in control. By controlling the stormy seas, and a great fish, God displayed his absolute, yet loving guidance.

Rather than running from God, we need to run to God and trust Him with your past, present, and future. Saying no to God quickly leads to disaster; saying yes to God brings new understanding and His purpose in the world. Just say yes to God and His will for you.

God had a purpose for Jonah – to preach the great Assyrian city of Nineveh. Do you know your purpose? Jonah hated Nineveh, and so he responded with anger and indifference. Jonah had yet to learn that God loves all

people; He hates the sin but loves us. Though Jonah, God reminded Israel of their missionary purpose.

God wants His people to proclaim His love in words and actions to the whole world. He wants us to be His missionaries where ever we are and where ever He sends us, so stop crying and get up, and get going.

CHAPTER 2

STRUGGLING WITH ADDICTIONS

My cousin was struggling with an addiction, and he knew it. His friends and family members encouraged him to stop. He agreed that it would be best for his health and relationships, but he felt helpless. When others told him how they had quit their bad habits, he replied: "I'm happy for you, but I can't seem to stop! I wish I had never been tempted in the first place." He was crying out for help and is still crying for help after thirty (30) something years.

Immediate deliverance may happen for some, but most face a daily battle. While we don't always understand why the temptation doesn't go away, we can turn to God or whatever path we find ourselves! Perhaps that is most important part of our struggle. We learn to exchange our futile efforts to change for complete dependence on God, who hears our cry for help. (Psalm 34:17) – "The righteous cry and the Lord heareth and delivereth them out of all their troubles." Jesus was tempted also, just as we are, so He understands what we are feeling; (Mark 1:13) – "And He was there in the wilderness forty days, tempted of Satan; and was with the wild beasts; and the angels ministered unto him."

Yes that is what we need, ministering to. He sympathizes with our struggles. (Hebrews 4:15-16) – "For we have not an high priest which cannot be touched with

the feeling of our infirmities; but was in all points tempted like as we are, yet without sin. Let us therefore come boldly unto the throne of grace that we may obtain mercy, and find grace to help in time of need." He also uses others, including trained professionals, to lean on along the way.

Whatever battles we may be facing today, we know this - God loves us much more than we can imagine, and He is faithful to come to our assistance. (I Corinthians 10:11-13) – Now all these events happen to them as examples for us, they were written down to warn us, who live at the time when this age was drawing to a close. If you think you are standing strong, be careful, for you too, may fall into the same sin. But remember that the temptations that come into your life are no different from what others experience. And God is faithful. He will keep the temptation from becoming so strong that you can't stand up against it. When you are tempted, He will show you a way out so that you will not give in to it.

In a culture filled with moral depravity and pressures, Paul gave strong encouragement to the Corinthians about temptation. He said (1) wrong derives and temptations happen, so don't feel you've been singled out, (2) others have resisted temptation so you can, (3) any temptation can be resisted because God will help you resist it, God helps you resist the temptation by helping you recognize people and situations that give you trouble. Run from anything you know is wrong, choose to do only what is right, pray for God's help, and put friends who love God and can offer help

in times of temptation. Running from a tempting situation is the first step to victory.

Joseph having to run is in 39th chapter of Genesis. (Genesis 39:9) – Potiphar's wife failed to seduce Joseph, who resisted this temptation by saying it would be a sin against God. How many of us take out time to think about God at a time of temptation? Joseph didn't say "I'd be hurting you or I'd be sinning against Potiphar" or "I'd be sinning against myself." Under pressure, such excuses are easily rationalized away. Remember that sexual sin is not just between two consenting adults, it is an act of disobedience to God.

Joseph avoided Potiphar's wife as much as possible, he refused her advances and finally ran away from her. Sometimes merely trying to avoid temptation is not enough. We have to turn and run, especially when the temptation is so strong, as is often the case with sexual temptation, don't think about it – run, run, run.

"Do not love the world or the things in the world. If anyone loves the world, the love of the Father is not in him. For all that is in the world, the lust of the flesh, the lust of the eyes, and the pride of life, is not of the Father but is of the world. And the world is passing away, and the lust of it; but he who does the will of God abides forever." (1 John 2:15–17)

"Dearly beloved, I beseech you as strangers and pilgrims abstain from fleshly lusts, which war against the soul." (1 Peter 2:11)

"For all that is in the world, the desires of the flesh and the desires of the eyes and pride in possessions, is not from the Father, but is from the world." (1 John 2:16)

"Now the works of flesh are manifest, which are these; Adultery, fornication, uncleanness, lasciviousness (pornography), Idolatry (extreme admiration, love, reference of something or someone), witchcraft, hatred, variance (conflicting, the state or fact of disagreeing, quarreling, fighting, deviation), emulations (contest, strife, competition, rivalry accompanied with the desire of depressing another), wrath, envying, murders, drunkenness, and suchlike: of which I tell you before, as I have told you in time past, that they which do such things shall not inherit the kingdom of God." (Galatians 5:19-21)

"Be not deceived: evil communications corrupt good manners." (1 Corinthians 15:33)

You see anything that enslaves you causes you to be its servant, drawing you away from God. Those things keep you from serving God and being there for and fellowshipping with His people that need you in their lives or maybe you need them in your life. The bible warns us that those who continue to do those things will not enter the kingdom of God, and there is a way to be freed from our addictions by allowing the Holy Spirit to work in and through us.

CHAPTER 3

HOW LONG SHALL I WAIT

Psalm 13:1-6 – "How long wilt thou forget me, O Lord? Forever? How long wilt thou hide thy face from me? How long shall I take counsel in my soul, having sorrow in my heart daily? How long shall my enemy be exalted over me? Consider and hear me O Lord my God; lighten mine eyes, lest I sleep the sleep of death; lest mine enemy say, I have prevailed against him; and those that trouble me rejoice when I am moved. But I have trusted in thy mercy; my heart shall rejoice in thy salvation. I will sing unto the Lord, because he hath dealt bountifully with me."

Waiting is hard at times; but when days, weeks and months pass and our prayers seem to go unanswered, it's easy to feel God has forgotten us. Perhaps we can struggle through the day with its distractions, but at night it's doubly difficult to deal with our anxious thoughts.

Worries seem large, and the dark hours loom endless. Utter weariness makes it look impossible to face the new day. The psalmist grew weary as he waited as in Psalm 13:1. He felt abandoned as if his enemies were gaining the upper hand. When we're waiting for God to help resolve a difficult problem or to answer often – repeated prayers; it's easy to get discouraged. Satan whispers that God has forgotten us and that things will never change. We may be

tempted to give in to despair, why bother to read the Bible or even to pray?

Why make the effort to worship with other believers in Christ? But we need our spiritual believers most when we're waiting. They help to hold us steady in flow of God's love and to become sensitive to His spirit. That is why we can cry for help, He'll be there. God is worth waiting for. His time is always best.

Delay does not mean denial. Time spent waiting on God is never wasted. When Jesus heard that Lazarus was sick, He waited two more days in the place where he was.

John 11:7-35: In verses 7-11 – "Jesus said Let us go into Judaea again, the disciples said that where the Jews sought to stone thee, Jesus answered, Are there not twelve hours in the day? If any man walk in the day, he stumbleth not, because he seeth the light of this world but if a man walk in the night he stumbleth, because there is not light in him. Our friend Lazarus sleepeth, but I go, that I may awake him out of sleep."

John 11:23 –"Jesus said unto her, thy brother shall rise again".

John 11:25 – "Jesus said unto her, I am the resurrection, and the life; he that believeth in me, though he was dead, yet shall he live."

John11:26 – "And whosoever liveth and believeth in me shall never die. Believeth thou this?" Jesus told Lazarus to come forth, then commanded them to loose him, and let him go. There are miracles and blessings in waiting.

Psalm 25:5 – "Lead me in thy truth, and teach me; for thou art the God of my salvation; on thee do I wait all the day."

Proverbs 20:22 – "Say not thou, I will recompense evil, but wait on the Lord, and he shall save thee."

Isaiah 8:17 – "I will wait upon the Lord………..

Lamentations 3:25 – "The Lord is good unto them that wait for him, to the soul that seeketh him."

Hosea 12:6 – "Therefore turn thou to thy God, keep mercy and judgment, and wait on thy God continually."

I Thessalonians 1:10 – "And to wait for his son from heaven."

CHAPTER 4

CRYBABY BLUES

Crying is all about feelings. Overcome depression with the help of God and His Holy Spirit. Depression is often triggered by life circumstances, such as a loss of job, death of a loved one, divorce, or psychological problems such as abuse or low self-esteem. The Bible tells us to be filled with joy and praise. (Philippians 4:4) – "Rejoice in the Lord always; and again I say, Rejoice."

(Romans 15:11) – "And again Praise the Lord, all ye Gentiles, and land him, all ye people." So, God apparently intends for us all to live joyful lives. Depression is a widespread condition, affecting millions of people, Christians, and non-Christians alike. Those suffering from depression can experience intense feelings of sadness, much crying, anger, hopelessness, fatigue, and a variety of other symptoms. They may begin to feel useless and suicidal, losing interest in things and people that they once enjoyed.

This is not easy for someone suffering from situational depression, but it can be remedied through God's gift of prayer, Bible study, and application, support groups, fellowship among believers, confession, forgiveness, and counseling. We must make the conscious effort to not be absorbed in ourselves, but to turn our efforts outward. Feelings of depression can often be solved when those suffering with depression move the focus from themselves

to Christ and others. Stay in the Word, even when you don't feel like it.

Emotions can lead us astray, but God's Word stands firm and unchanging. We must maintain strong faith in God and hold even more tightly to Him when we undergo trials and temptations into our lives that we can not bear. 1 Corinthians 10:13 " There hath no temptation taken you but such as is common to man; but God is faithful, who will not suffer you to be tempted above that ye are able; but will with the temptation also make a way to escape, that ye may be able to bear it."

Being depressed is not a sin, (Hebrew 13:15) - "Through Jesus therefore, let us continually offer to God a sacrifice of praise – the fruit of our life that confess his name." Elijah and the problem of depression are in 1 Kings 19. In James 5:17 – Remember Elijah, he was a man like us. Elijah's experiences were the same as ours. He had difficulties. He had tests. He knew what depression was like. Our enemy, the devil, was depression, God helps us. Elijah was tired – that's when the devil tries to attack us, when our bodies feel very tired and weak. Elijah sat down under a tree and wanted to die. He had no physical energy at the time.

(1 Kings 18:46) He had run nearly twenty (20) miles to a place called Jezreel. Then he heard bad news in the city. So, he ran for more than another eighty (80) miles. He was very tired and depressed. When you hear bad news, it's no surprise to feel depressed. Elijah had great experiences on the mountain. (1 Kings 18:16-39) God had showed his

power and greatness. Elijah must have felt great excitement. He was so happy, and then came depression. The devil wants to steal from us. He wants to take away our joy and peace in God. He tries to make us forget about God and His goodness toward us. It comes when we least expect it. He (God) provides help; Elisha is an example of this. In 1 Kings 19:19-21, God gave him to Elijah. He poured water on the hands of Elijah. In 2 Kings 3:11 it means that he served Elijah.

God is very good to us too. He usually sends someone into our lives. That one will poor water over our dirty, tired hands. He or she will help and encourage us. God shall wipe away all your tears. Revelations 21:4

No more wah, wah, wah, wah

CHAPTER 5

HELP IS ON THE WAY

There are times in our lives when we feel like we're stuck in a really bad place, we're crying help. Anxious and alone, we despair that we are out of options and that no one under ft ands where we really are in life. But in such moments we need to remember God's comforting words to the early Christians who were stuck in a world where Satan's presence dominated all that was around them. "I know thy works, and where thou dwellest, even where Satan's seat is: and thou holdest fast thy name, and hast not denied my faith, even in those days wherein Antipas was my faithful martyr, who was slain among you, where Satan dwelleth." (Revelation 2:13)

Their situation had not escaped the heavenly Father's notice. And as they were faithful to Him, He would sustain them until He rescued them and brought them safely home. The fact that God knows where you are and that He is very much aware of the difficult situations you are in and provides the confidence and strength needed to live for His glory. So be encouraged. Remember God's words of comfort. Help is on the way.

You know the struggles that we face Lord. You know just what we need to endure them. Give us the confidence we need to trust you because of your goodness and to walk by faith. Amen.

Our greatest hope here below is help from God above. What once was normal may never be normal again. So the challenge for those offering help is to assist the sufferers as they establish the normal. It may be a new normal that no longer includes robust health, a treasured relationship, or a satisfying job. It may be living without a loved one who has been taken in death but help is still on the way.

It's easy to think that no one understands how we feel. But that isn't true. Part of the reason that Jesus came was to experience life among us, resulting in His present ministry. "For we do not have a High Priest who cannot sympathize with our weaknesses, but was in all points tempted as we are, yet without sin." (Hebrews 4:15)

Our Saviour lived a perfect life, yet He also knew the pains of a broken world. He endured sorrow; He suffered agony. He stands ready to encourage us when the dark moments of life force us to embrace a new normal. In our desert of grief, Jesus can provide an oasis of hope.

(2 Corinthians 11:30) – "If I must boast, I will boast in the things which concern my infirmity." The apostle Paul suffered all sorts of hardships as he pursued his goals of sharing the good news of Jesus with those who had never heard. Persecuted, beaten, imprisoned, and misunderstood, sometimes he faced death itself. (2 Corinthians 11:25) But the joy of seeing people respond to his message made it all worth while. If you feel that the task God has called you to do is hard, remember that the spiritual lessons and joy that are wrapped up in the journey may seem hidden at first, but they are certainly there! God will help you find them.

Nehemiah 6:9 - "Now therefore, O God, strengthen my hands."

Nehemiah, who led in the rebuilding of the wall of Jerusalem, refused to give up. He faced insults and intimidation from the enemies all around him as well as injustices from his own people. (Nehemiah chapters 4-5) His enemies even insinuated that he had a personal agenda. (Nehemiah 6:6-7) He sought help fro God while taking every defensive step he could.

Despite the challenges, the wall was completed in 52 days. (Nehemiah 6:15) But Nehemiah work was not complete. He encouraged the Israelites to study the scriptures to worship, and to keep God's law, after completing 12 years of governor in (Nehemiah 5:14). He returned to make sure his reforms were continuing in (Nehemiah 13:6). Nehemiah had a life-long commitment to leading the people. We all face challenges and difficulties in life. But as God helped Nehemiah, He will also help us by strengthening our hands in (Nehemiah 6:9), for the rest of our lives in whatever tasks he gives us.

Life's challenges are made not to break us but to bend us toward God. (Philippians 2:1-2) - "If there be therefore any consolation in Christ, if any comfort of love, if any fellowship of the Spirit, if any bowels and mercies. Fulfill ye my joy, that ye be likeminded, having the same love, being of one accord, of one mind." (Jude 1:24-25) "Now unto him that is able to keep you from falling, and to present you faultless before the presence of his glory with exceeding joy. To the only wise God our Saviour, be

glory and majesty, dominion and power, both now and ever. Amen!" (Psalm 121:1-2) – "I will lift up mine eyes unto the hills, from whence cometh my help. My help cometh from the Lord, which made heaven and earth."

Scriptures that will help you thru anything; (Hebrews 4:16) – "Let us therefore come boldly unto the throne of grace, that we may obtain mercy, and find grace to help in time of need." (Psalm 46:1-2) – "God is our refuge and strength, a very present help in trouble. Therefore will not we fear, though the earth be removed, and though the mountains be carried into the midst of the sea." (Romans 10: 9-10) – "That if thou shalt confess with thy mouth the Lord Jesus, and shalt believe in thine heart that God hath raised him from the dead, thou shalt be saved. For with thine heart man believeth unto righteousness; and with the mouth confession is made unto salvation." Proverbs 30:5 – "Every word of God is pure; he is a shield unto them that put their trust in him."

Crying makes 9 out of 10 people feel better, reduces stress, and may help to keep the body healthy. Cry your eyes out. (Psalm 22:2, 5, and 19) – "O my God, I cry in the daytime, but thou hearest not; and in the night season, and am not silent." "They cried unto thee, and were delivered: they trusted in thee, and were not confounded." "But be not thou far from me, O Lord: O my strength, haste thee to help me." (Psalm 6:8-9) – Depart from me, all ye workers of iniquity; for the Lord hath heard the voice of my weeping. The Lord hath heard my supplication; the Lord will receive my prayer."

CRY HELP THRU RELATIONSHIPS

We have been through several different relationships with family members, co-workers, with boyfriend and girlfriend, with husband and wife, and with church members. But the most important relationship is with God. (Notice I didn't mention friend, far and between) The Old Testament story of Joseph follows a favorite son whose brothers hated him in Genesis chapters 37- 50.

Do you have family members that dislike you and mistreat you for no reason what so ever? Family members are the worst ones, Jesus said that His family members did not receive Him. Joseph refused to build a wall of hatred between himself and his brothers, who sold him into slavery when a famine brought them face to face after many years. Joseph treated his brothers with kindness saying, "You meant evil against me but God meant it for my good. And he comforted them and spoke kindly to them." (Genesis 50:20-21) He was helping to restore the relationship between them.

If we've built walls of anger in separation between ourselves and others, the Lord is willing and able to help us begin tearing them down today. Anger builds walls, love breaks them down. (Genesis 50:21) - "He confronted them and spoke kindly to them." The Bible teaches us to avoid angry outbursts by putting on the new self, "which

was created according to God; in true righteousness and holiness," in Ephesians 4:24. If we are the victim of anger; God asks us to "be kind to one another, tenderhearted, forgiving one another, even as Christ forgave you." (Ephesians 4:32)

Restoring relationships are not easy, but they are possible by the grace of God. I remember back in the days my sisters and I use to fight each other, but also use to take up for each other when we got into fights with someone else outside of family. We would make up, because we were sisters. There's an old cliché that says "the best things in life are free." There's a lot of truth in that. Some people believe that the best things in life are expensive and/or exclusive.

However, the best things in life are not things. The value of family, friends, and faith points us to the realization that what matters most in life is all wrapped up in people and the Lord. Solomon was well qualified to speak about material things because he "surpassed all the kings of the earth in riches and wisdom," and this is found in (1 kings 10:23). Do not overwork to be rich, because of your own understanding, Cease! Will you set your eyes on that which is not? For riches certainly make themselves wings; they fly away like an eagle towards heaven." (Proverbs 23:4-5)

(Proverbs 23:12, 18) – "Apply your heart to instruction, and your eyes to words of knowledge. For surely there is a here after, and your hope will not be cut off." The best things in life are eternal riches that come from God's goodness and grace in Jesus. Christ. We do not hold them in our hands, but in our hearts.

"A good relationship is more than something we want - it's something we need to be our happiest, healthiest, and most productive selves. But at home or work, supportive and fulfilling relationships don't come automatically. They take an investment in time and energy as well as social skills that can be learned." We need each other to survive.

The first thing we need to do before entering any relationship is to find ourselves. Let us take a look in the mirror, who do we see? Seeing ourselves on camera or in the mirror and keep us focused on outward appearances and leave us with little interest in examining our inner selves. Self-examination is crucial for a healthy spiritual life. God wants us to see ourselves so that we can be spared the consequences of sinful choices.

(1 Corinthians 11:23-28)- "For I have received of the Lord that which also I delivered unto you, that the Lord Jesus the same night in which he was betrayed and took bread. And when he had given thanks, he broke it and said Take, eat: this is my body, which is broken for you: this do in remembrance of me. After the same manner also he took the cup, when he had supped, saying, This cup is the New Testament in my blood: this do ye, as oft as ye drink it, in remembrance of me. For as often as ye eat this bread, and drink this cup, ye do shew the Lord's death till he come. Wherefore whosoever shall eat this bread, and drink this cup of the Lord, unworthily, shall be guilty of the body and blood of the Lord. But let a man examine himself, and so let him eat of that bread, and drink of that cup."

The basis of this examination of self is not only to make things right with God but also to make sure we are right with one another. The Lord's Supper is a remembrance of Christ's body, and we can't celebrate it properly if we're not living in harmony with are other believers. Seeing and confessing our sins promote unity with others and a great relationship with God. When we look into the mirror of God's Word, we see ourselves clearly.

Dear Lord, help me to be more concerned with the reflection of my heart than with my physical reflection. Change me through the power of your spirit; if you find anything in me that is not good in your sight, take it out and strengthen me, I surrender.

The Bible tells us that our greatest need is not simply guidance in life but it's a relationship with God. The most defining moment in anyone's life is the decision to surrender to God by accepting Christ as our personal Saviour. We will eventually experience different types of relationships. Co-dependent relationship, you and your partner (or both of you) cannot function without the other person. Independent relationship, is when you put yourself a head of your partner and vice versa, your highly focused on your careers or your own lives, you are two people who do not know how or are not willing to compromise and sacrifice for the relationship. Dominating relationship is when you'll date someone who controls you. They will set all rules for the relationship, and you will follow them. Rebound relationship is when you have just gone through a breakup and need love to cover up the pain. This relationship almost never works out

because it is built on the fear of facing the reality of your recent breakup; your focus is not on the new person. It's over wah, wah, wah.

Open relationship, in this the two persons are emotionally committed to one another, but are free to see other people. It's ended boo hoo hoo. A Toxic relationship will leave you feeling emotionally, mentally and physically immobile. One in which you and your partner have an extreme attraction to one another, but have such different morals, opinion, or integrity that all you do is fight. You bring out the worse and each other. Another relationship Purely sexual-basically friend type, this relationship is purely sexual. When you call or text one another, it's almost always to spend time immediately. You are mostly in the bedroom together. These are just a few unhealthy relationships.

(Philemon 1:16) - Not now as a servant, but above a servant, a brother beloved, specially to me, but how much more unto thee, both in the flesh, and in the Lord? Onesimus was a runaway slave who had escaped from his Christian master Philemon. Onesimus had come to faith through Paul's ministry, and now Paul was sending him back to Philemon with these words "perhaps he departed for a while for this purpose, that you might receive Him forever, no longer as a slave more than a slave - a beloved brother found in verses 15-16.

When people leave your church and come back let's receive them in love. Although we don't know if Onesimus was set free from slavery, his new faith in Jesus had changed

his relationship with his Christian master. He was now also a brethren in Christ. Paul was influencing his world one heart at a time. By transforming power of the gospel, people and situations can change. The kindest thing you can do for another is to show him the truth. Jesus is the way, the truth and the light. (Matthew 5:9) – "Blessed are the peacemaker, for they shall be called Sons of God."

Song: "I have the peace that passes understanding down in my heart__ down in my heart to stay!"

The peace of God is truly a gift we enjoy in our hearts as we fellowship in his presence (John 14:27). Peace is a gift we need to share with others. In Jesus sermon on the mountain, he said "Blessed are the peacemakers." found in (Matthew 5:9), which indicates that we need to bring peace to our relationships. Peacemakers are those who turn the other cheek Matthew 5:39, go the extra mile in Matthew 5:41, and love their enemies while praying for those who persecute them in Matthew 5:44. Because of the peace of God and peace with God, we can be peacemakers for God so are we the sons of God.

Matthew 18:33 – "Should you not also have compassion on your fellow servant, just as I had pity on you." The gospel of Jesus Christ brings the promise of peace and reconciliation with God and with each other. When Peter asked Jesus how often he should forgive a brother who sinned against him. (Matthew 18:31) The Lord surprised everyone by saying "seventy times seven" in a day. Then he told an on forgettable story about a servant who had received forgiveness but didn't pass it on.

As God freely forgives us, we also should forgive others. With God's love and power, forgiveness is always possible. Nothing is impossible with God. (Philippians 2:3) – "Let nothing be done through selfish ambition or conceit." In (Philippians 4:2), Paul wrote to 2 women in the church saying "I implore Euodias and Syntyche to be of the same mind in the Lord. A quarrel between these two women threatened to tear down the witness of the Philippians church if left unresolved. So Paul urges true companion to help rebuild that relationship. We do quarrel but we should seek to "live a peaceably" with all. Romans 12:18

It takes much effort and time to reconcile broken relationships. But it's worth it. We should seek to build each other up through our words and actions. Peace! There was one of my boys that hated to apologize, instead of saying I'm sorry he would just stand there and cry for minutes to almost an hour, what a sad situation. I guess he didn't think he did anything wrong, but even I knew that we still need to apologize.

(Matthew 5:23-24) – "Therefore if thou bring thy gift to the altar, and there rememberest that thy brother hath ought against thee; Leave there thy gift before the altar, and go thy way; first be reconciled to thy brother, and then come and off thy gift."

Apologies are needed in our relationships. Apologizing is a biblical action. Jesus instructed His followers to make things right with those we've offended. And the Apostle Paul said "If it is possible, as much as

depends on you live peaceably with all." Living at peace may require apologies. Apologies can be hard to make because it takes a spirit of humility to admit our mistakes, which may not come naturally for us. But taking responsibility for how we wrong in a situation can bring healing and restoration to a relationship. Have you made a mistake? Swallow your pride and apologize. Even if you have to cry still apologize.

CHAPTER 7

LET THE SON SHINE IN

Jesus said to His followers you are "The light of the world." (Matthew 5:14) John wrote that Christ is the true light "Shines in the darkness." (John 1:5) Jesus gives invitation to us to reflect our light into the darkness around us. "Let your light shine before others, that they may see your good deeds and glorify your Father in heaven." (Matthew 5:16) That is a call for us to show love in the face of hatred, patience in times of trouble, and peace in the midst of confusion. Paul reminds us, "For you were once darkness, but now you are light in the Lord, Live as children of light." (Ephesians 5:8)

Jesus said "I am the light of the world. Whosoever follows me will never walk in darkness, but will have the light of life." (John 8:12) Our light is a reflection of Jesus the Son. Reflect the Son and shine for Him.

Psalm 121 – "I will lift up mine eyes unto the hills, from whence cometh my <u>help</u>. My <u>help</u> cometh from the Lord, which made heaven and earth. He will not suffer thy foot to be moved; he that keepeth thee will not slumber. Behold, he that keepeth Israel shall neither slumber, nor sleep. The Lord is thy keeper; the Lord is the shade upon thy right hand. The sun shall not smite thee by day, nor the moon by night. The Lord shall preserve thee from all evil; he shall preserve thy soul. The Lord shall preserve thy

going out and thy coming in from this time forth, and even for evermore."

(Romans 8:3-4)- "For what the law could not do, in that it was weak through the flesh, God sending his own Son in the likeness of sinful flesh, and for sin, condemned sin in flesh: That the righteousness of the law might be fulfilled in us, who walk not after the flesh, but after the spirit."

God sent His own Son into the world so Man can have a right to the tree of life.

John 1:18 – "No man hath seen God at any time, the only begotten, Son which is in the bosom of the Father, he hath declared him." Jesus is now sitting on the right hand of the Father. (John 3:16-17) – "For God so loved the world, that He gave His only begotten Son, that whosoever believeth in him should not perish, but have everlasting life. For God sent not his Son into the world to condemn the world; but the world through him might be saved."

If you are not saved and want to be all you have to do is confess with your mouth to the Lord Jesus who was raised from the dead and believe what it is that you're saying from your heart and you will be saved, simple as that but you are going to have to make some changes.

Salvation is as close as your own heart and mouth. People think it must be a complicated process, but it's not. Sometimes we like people, try to get right with God by keeping His laws. We may think Church attendance, Church work, giving offerings, and being nice will be

enough. After all, we've played by the rules, haven't we? But Paul's words sting - this approach never succeeds. Paul explains that God's plan is not for us to try to earn his favor by being good.

It is for those who realize they can never be good enough and so we must depend totally on Christ. Only by putting our faith in what Jesus Christ has done will we be saved. If we do that, we will never be put to shame, because Christ went to the cross and died for our sins, what a God we serve. He hung, bled and died, and then rose again so we to can rise again with new life in Christ of Hope of Glory. Amen.

CHAPTER 8

MY TESTIMONY

This is my testimony on how good God is to me. I went in for shortness of breath to the emergency room within two hours they asked my husband had he realized how sick I was, then they rushed me to ICU, where they found that I had pneumonia and a clot in my lung. Within 4 hours of being in ICU, I had a stroke on the right side and lost activity of my right leg, and right hand. I couldn't talk; my husband said he called the nurse because nothing was moving. He said the nurse said I had brain damage on the left side that affected the right side of my body, and I went into cardiac arrest three times.

I was at DeKalb Medical Hospital at Hillandale for a month and a half on a breathing machine (life support). After a month and a half, they said I was only living by the machine; they spoke with my husband to put a trachea in my throat. They got my husband to sign paperwork off on the procedure. When they got ready to take me to put in the trachea, that was my miracle starting. God is a healer. I am a witness. The doctors said my breathing was higher than the machine. They took me off the machine and I was immediately placed in a regular room.

One week later I was transported to DeKalb Medical Hospital on Church Street in Decatur, Ga. for the rehab. They said that it would take me about 6 weeks to 1 year to

recover, but God did another miracle. It took me 2 weeks, I started working better, talking better, and using my right hand better. I went to physical, occupational and speech therapy. What a mighty God we serve.

After two weeks in therapy they released me. I went to church the next week, not in a wheelchair, not on crutches. I walked in the church with my high heel shoes on and ran around the church. Christmas morning they wanted to take me off the machine and let me go. My husband refused to take me off, that would not have been a good Christmas gift. But I thank God for the gift of life. I have New life in Christ. Thank you, Jesus. My husband said they wanted to give me a trachea to stop me from preaching, what the devil meant for bad, God turned it around for my good.

Thank you, Jesus!

CHAPTER 9

CRYING TO JESUS (GOD)

Scriptures states that there is a time to cry and everyone will cry at some point or another in life. The world say things like men ought not to cry, but in the Bible you see the strongest people crying out to God.

Jesus who is God himself cried (John 11:35) "Jesus wept". When Jesus friend Lazarus died his sister John 11:32-35 "Then when Mary was come where Jesus was, and saw him, she fell down at his feet, saying unto him, Lord, if thou hadst been here, my brother had not died. When Jesus therefore saw her crying (weeping), and the Jews also weeping which came with her, he groaned in the spirit, and was troubled, and said, Where have ye laid him? They said unto him, Lord, come and see. Jesus wept."

Here are some scriptures of men crying in the bible:

Genesis 27:38 - "And Esau said unto his father, "Do you have only one blessing, my father? Bless me too, my father!" Then Esau **wept** aloud.

Genesis 29:11 - "And Jacob kissed Rachel, and lifted up his voice and **wept**."

Genesis 42:24 - "And he turned himself about from them, and **wept**; and returned to them again, and

took communed with them Simeon, and bound him before their eyes."

Genesis 43:30 – "Deeply moved at the sight of his brother, Joseph hurried out and looked for a place to **weep**. He went into his private room and **wept** there."

Genesis 45:14 – "Then he threw his arms around his brother Benjamin and **wept**, and Benjamin embraced him, **weeping**."

Genesis 45:15 – "And he kissed all his brothers and **wept** over them. Afterward his brothers talked with him."

1 Samuel 30:4 – "So David and his men **wept** aloud until they had no strength left to **weep**."

2 Samuel 1:12 – "They mourned and **wept** and fasted till evening for Saul and his son Jonathan, and for the army of the Lord and the house of Israel, because they had fallen by the sword."

2 Samuel 15:30 – "But David continued up the Mount of Olives, **weeping** as he went; his head was covered and he was barefoot. All the people with him covered their heads too and were **weeping** as they went up."

2 Samuel 18:33 – "The king was shaken. He went up to the room over the gateway and **wept**. As he went, he said: "O my son Absalom! My son, my

son Absalom! If only I had died instead of you – O Absalom, my son, my son!"

2 Kings 20:3 "Remember, O Lord, how I have walked before you faithfully and with wholehearted devotion and have done what is good in your eyes." And Hezekiah **wept** bitterly.

2 Kings 20:5 "Go back and tell Hezekiah, the leader of my people, 'This is what the Lord, the God of your father David, says: I have heard your prayer and seen your **tears**; I will heal you. On the third day from now you will go up to the temple of the Lord.

2 Chronicles 34:27 – "Because your heart was responsive and you humbled yourself before God when you heard what he spoke against this place and its people, and because you humbled yourself before me and tore your robes and **wept** in my presence, I have heard you, declares the Lord."

Psalms 6:6 – "I am worn out from groaning; all night long I flood my bed with **weeping** and drench my couch with **tears**."

Micah 1:8 – "Because of this I will **weep** and **wail**; I will go about barefoot and naked. I will howl like a jackal and moan like an owl."

2 Corinthians 2:4 – "For I wrote you out of great distress and anguish of heart and with many **tears**,

not to grieve you but to let you know the depth of my love for you."

Revelation 5:4 – "I **wept** and **wept** because no one was found who was worthy to open the scroll or look inside."

When you feel sad about anything the best thing to do is to cry out to the Lord and pray and He will guide you and help you. From experience if you go to God with your problems He will give you a peace and comfort unlike any other feeling. We should cry on God's shoulder in prayer. Crying doesn't mean you're weak it means you have a heart. In Psalm 56:8-9 "Thou tellest my wanderings: put thou my tears into thy bottle: are they not in thy book? When I cry unto thee, then shall mine enemies turn back; this I know; for God is for me." If God be for you, who can be against you.

Psalm 107:19- "Then they cry unto the Lord in their trouble, and he saveth them out their distresses." Have you ever cried out to the Lord and He heard and answered your prayer? He's just that good. What an Awesome God we serve. In Psalm 34:17 - "The righteous cry out, and the Lord hears them, He delivers them from all their troubles." Psalm 107:6 - "Then they cried out to the Lord in there troubles, and he delivered them from their distresses."

I remember when my son Mario was shot by a drive by shooting, he was in bad state. He was lying in the hospital bed dead for 56 days, yes I said dead. Me and several other ministers went to the side of his bed, oiled him down from

his head to his feet, and cried to God for help and the Lord heard our Cry and answered us for his life. He came back and the bullet is still inside of him till this day, but he is still here by the Grace of God. And my son Donta also went through an ordeal where he had to go in the hospital. The doctors said he wouldn't live, but God and he is still here, Praise the Lord, so if you think crying is foolish then think again. I will continue to cry to the Lord for my children and our members and He will deliver.

Another instance I remember when they said my son Timothy also known as Pooh, was stabbed. We immediately began to cry out to God and He heard our cry, and our son was released from the hospital the next day. Tell me what you think? I think that when you are real with God and have a calling on your life, there is nothing you can say or do to stop God from doing what He has to do. I believe all of our children have a calling on their lives that is the why the devil attacks them so, but God is still able to do exceedingly, abundantly, and above all we can ask or think. Psalm 37:5 - "Commit everything you do to the Lord, trust Him, and He will help you." Psalm 46:1 - Says "God is our protection and source of strength. He is always ready to help us in times of trouble."

Isaiah 41:10 - "Fear not, for I am with you, be not dismayed, for I am your God, I will strengthen you, I will help you, I will uphold you with my righteous right hand." (James 1:2-4) - "Consider it pure joy, my brothers and sisters, whenever you face trouble of many kinds, because you know that the testing of your faith produces

perseverance. Let perseverance finish its work so that you may be mature and complete, not lacking anything." Trust God and continue to pray and have faith. (1 Peter 5:7) – "Turn all your anxiety over to God because He cares for you." (Genesis 4:9-10) - "And the Lord said unto Cain, Where is Abel thy brother? And he said, I know not: Am I my brother's keeper? And he said, What hast thou done? the voice of thy brother's blood crieth on to me from the ground."

Explained in Genesis chapter 4, Cain was upset with Abel because Cain brought of the fruit of the ground an offering unto the Lord, and Abel brought of the firstlings of his flock and the fat thereof. And the Lord had respect unto able and to his offering because he gave his best, but Cain and to his offering he had not respect.

Psalm 27:7 - "Hear, O Lord, when I cry with my voice; have mercy also upon me, and answer me." (Psalm 39:12) – "Hear my prayer, O Lord, and give ear unto my cry; hold not thy peace at my tears: for I am a stranger with thee, and a sojourner, as all my fathers were." (Psalm 18:6) - "In my distress I called upon the Lord, and cried and unto my God; he heard my voice out of his temple, and my cry came before him even into his ears."

1 Samuel 1:10 - "Hannah was in deep anguish, crying bitterly as she prayed to the Lord."

(Psalm 106:44) – "Nevertheless he regarded their affliction, when he heard their cry."

John 20:11-15 - "But Mary stood outside the tomb weeping. As she wept, she bent down and looked into the tomb. And she saw two angels and white sitting where Jesus body had been lying, one at the head and one at the feet. They said to her, "Woman, why are you weeping?" Mary replied, "They have taken my lord away, and I do not know where they have put him." When she had said this, she turned around and saw Jesus standing there, but she did not know that it was Jesus. Jesus said to her, "Woman, why are you crying? Who are you looking for?" Because she thought he was the gardener, she said to him, "Sir, if you have carried him away, tell me where you have put him, and I will take him."

Isaiah 19:20 – "And it shall be for a sign and for a witness unto the Lord of hosts in the land of Egypt: for they shall cry unto the Lord because of the oppressors, and he shall send them a Saviour, and a great one, and he shall deliver them." (Psalm 31:22) – "In my alarm I said, I am cut off from your sight!" Yet you heard my cry for mercy when I called to you for help." David cried to the Lord on several occasions.

Psalm 28 – "Unto thee will I cry, O Lord my rock; be not silent to me: lest, if thou be silent to me, I become like them that go down into the pit. Hear the voice of my supplications, when I cry unto thee, when I lift up my hands toward the holy oracle. Draw me not away with the wicked, and with the workers of iniquity, which speak peace to their neighbors, but mischief is in their hearts. Give them according to their deeds, and according to the wickedness

of their endeavours: give them after the work of their hands; render to them their desert. Because they regard not the works of the Lord, nor the operations of his hands, he shall destroy them, and not build them up. Blessed be the Lord, because he hath heard the voice of my supplications. The Lord is my strength and my shield: my heart trusted in him, and I am helped: therefore my heart greatly rejoiceth; and with my song will I praise him. The Lord is their strength, and he is the saving strength of his anointed. Save thy people, and bless thine inheritance: feed them also; and lift them up forever."

It's easy to pretend friendship; wicked people often masquerade in goodness, pretending kindness or friendship to gain their own ends. David, in his royal position, may have met many who pretended friendship for selfish reasons. David knew God would punish them accordingly, but he prayed that their punishment would come swiftly. True believers live honest lives before God and others.

Psalm 51 – Although David sinned with Bathsheba, he said he had sinned against God. When someone steals, murders, or slanders, it is against someone else – a victim. According to the world's standards, sex between two "consenting adults" is acceptable because nobody "gets hurt", but people do get hurt. In David's case, a man was murdered and a baby died. All sin hurts us and others, and ultimately it offends God because sin in any form is a rebellion against his way of living. When tempted to do wrong, remember that you will be sinning against God. That may help you stay on the right track.

Psalm 51:7-12 – "Purge me with hyssop, and I shall be clean: wash me, and I shall be whiter than snow. Make me to hear joy and gladness; that the bones which thou hast broken may rejoice. Hide thy face from my sins, and blot out all mine iniquities. Create in me a clean heart, O God; and renew a right spirit within me. Cast me not away from thy presence, and take not thy holy spirit from me. Restore unto me the joy of thy salvation; and uphold me with thy free spirit."

Hebrews 5:7 – "Who in the days of his flesh, when he had offered up prayers and supplications with strong crying in tears unto him that was able to save him from death, and was heard in that he feared." Jesus is our High Priest. (Hebrews 12:17) – "For ye know how that afterward, when he would have inherited the blessing, he was rejected; for he found no place of repentance, though he sought it carefully with tears." New Covenant. (Psalms 30:5) – "For his anger endureth but a moment; in his favour is life: weeping may endure for a night, but joy cometh in the morning.

Printed in the United States
By Bookmasters